Catstrology

The astro-guide to your pet's personality

Pat & Cat

MQP

Published by:
MQ Publications Limited
12 The Ivories
6–8 Northampton Street
London N1 2HY

tel: 020 7359 2244
fax: 020 7359 1616
email: mail@mqpublications.com
website: www.mqpublications.com

U.S. Office:
49 West 24th Streetç
8th Floor
New York
NY 10010
email: information@mqpublicationsus.com

Copyright © MQ Publications Limited 2005

Text © Patty Greenall and Cat Javor 2005

Design: Joy Lunn

ISBN: 1-84601-009-8

10 9 8 7 6 5 4 3 2 1

Printed and bound in China

Our Dedications

To SADIE the black and white Virgo, and to SABBATH the long-haired black Virgo

contents

introduction

As astrologers, we cat-loving authors have noticed that the zodiac sign of a cat is as much in evidence as with any human. You often ask your friends, "What's your sign?"; why not then ask your feline friends the same question?

OK, unless you're talking to a Gemini cat, you really have to ask its owner or someone who knows when it was born—but the reason for asking is the same. The zodiac can give you extra insight, so you can get to know your feline companion better. Even if you are uncertain of its precise date of birth, we feel sure that you'll recognize your cat in one of the 12 descriptions contained in this book. Astrology is a tool that is easily applied to the task of helping us to understand our pets, and there is more to it than meets the eye.

Like all other living creatures, each litter of kittens is born at a particular time; each kitten has its own astrological chart, and each will display unique traits that are characterized by the signs of the zodiac. While it's not easy to predict each and every feline life event, the different sun signs describe particular aspects of a cat's personality and behavior. Having said that, however, all cats share certain habits, and it's also accepted that there are certain character traits that are breed specific. Moreover, in astrology, all domestic animals are governed by the sixth house of the horoscope, so something else that all cats have in common is that they are considered to be of service to human beings. Within that category, there are further distinctions that need to be made. As much as you love your pet and want to treat it as an equal, a cat is a cat; it is not human, and you give the commands. But this is a two-way street, for when astrologers think about the sixth house with regard to pets, they not only think about how the service of our four-legged friends may help us practically, but also, how our association with them, and the various responsibilities we take for their care, can assist us to develop as more rounded, compassionate individuals. All cat lovers will tell you that, as domestic creatures, each one has its own personality, and affects its owner uniquely with its special character.

Further distinctions can be made about your cat depending on what time of the day it was born—one Taurus cat can seem very different from the next, just like humans. For instance, your cat may be displaying behavior more in keeping with its "ascendant" or "rising sign." The ascendant is the point on the eastern horizon at birth. In one period of 24 hours, all 12 signs of the zodiac will appear on that horizon, one after the other. The qualities of that rising sign are imprinted in the creature born at that moment. So although this book is about your cat's main sun sign, it's possible that it may be more closely aligned in character with its ascendant sign. So it's worth while reading through all 12 signs in order to determine which one is most like your cat. Some characteristics are very similar, and others are highly distinctive. You'll soon work it out. Have fun making up your mind!

Aries | The Leader

Aries

Suggested names for the Aries cat

Klaw, Rambo, Fez, Excalibur, Hagar, Hooligan, Bruiser, Spitfire, Bloody Mary, Boudicca, Topsy

Famous cat most likely to have been Aries

Thomas O'Malley

Enthusiastic

Impetuous

Energetic

Daring

Bright

The Aries cat is perhaps the most boisterous (some people say unruly) of all cats because it has such a strong need for independence combined with an insatiable interest in all things new. It has the ultimate "go for it" attitude. This is a cat with confidence, personality, and, it would seem, a belief that it can do whatever it wants, whenever it wants! So it's very determined. If some misguided person tries to stand in the way of an Aries cat, he or she will only ever do it once. Your Aries feline can even seem like a bit of a bully. It attacks life with a singular desire to conquer everything before it, lead the way, and generally let everybody know who is Top Cat.

When the Aries kitten or cat is first introduced to its new home, it will delight in scatting about the house at great speed, checking out and playing with every object in the place. It provides hours of fun for you with an endless supply of entertaining and precocious antics. It just seems so happy to be alive, in your company, and in your home. Be warned, however—your Aries kitty is setting you up with a false sense of security. Once it has conquered you and your territory, it may then march outdoors in order to set out to conquer the world. You could be forgiven for thinking that your mischievous little feline friend has run away from home! No, that's not what's happened. This part-time alley cat has only gone a little further afield than usual. It will probably be hanging out with the locals, letting them know that there's a new boss in town, or perhaps mingling with the neighbors, openly recruiting other humans to the personal army it's building. The Aries cat is not the kind of cat that will hide away or run from danger—in fact, sometimes it

11

might look as if it's spoiling for a fight. It's not scared of anything— it will tussle with other cats or even some larger animals that have had the audacity to wander into its territory. Given its penchant for getting into scraps, you won't be surprised that occasionally it will come back looking a little worse for wear. Don't lose sleep over it: more often than not, a lengthy absence will usually just mean that it's off doing its own thing. Moreover, if it can't be given freedom to come and go and finds that its roaming space is strictly limited to indoors, it's likely that your furniture and clothing will be tasted and tested frequently!

The Aries cat prefers fresh food, which means its very own catch of the day—so you can't be too squeamish! One thing is certain when you have an Aries cat around: the local mouse population will be kept under control. It's not really

that fussy about what you give it to eat. There may be days when it's ravenous and will mug you as soon as you walk in the door, and others when it's happy to go without because it just doesn't feel like eating the same thing again. It's best to offer it a variety, because the Aries cat is always attracted to anything new and exciting. And however much fun it gets from chasing down some tempting new prey, it is far less amusing for you to be picking up the discarded remains or carting your Aries kitty off to the veterinary clinic.

What is the Aries cat's favorite game? Cat and Mouse, of course! These prancing pouncers just relish a good chase. Whether it's a real mouse or just a piece of brightly colored string on the end of a stick, your Aries kitty will love it—at least for a few seconds! But once its attention is grabbed by something shinier or faster-moving, it will be off. Wind-up toys that make a noise and hurtle about the floor will provide your Aries cat with hours of fun and enjoyment.

You could buy it a fancy little cat basket, but the chances are that your Aries kitty will sleep wherever it happens to get tired—near a heater, by the television, on your bed, or anywhere it considers is most suitable at the time.

Unless you want a fight on your hands, it's easier and kinder to leave it be. This little warrior leads such an active life that it would be unfair and cruel to try to move it for anything other than an emergency. You might turn your Aries cat into a very insecure insomniac by regularly interrupting its sleep, because it always wakes wide-eyed, alert, and ready for action. A nervous Aries cat would be something of a liability—and hard on your nerves, too.

When you're looking for love and affection from your Aries cat, it is possible to misread the signs. This isn't the type of cat to delicately sidle up to you with a sweet meow and a gentle purr. It loves just as fiercely as it fights—and that can be rather disconcerting. You will be head-butted and pounced on, it will place a paw on each of your shoulders and lean against you with all its weight. It looks directly into your eyes, and when you're both face to face, it bares its teeth in a wide and open grin. Be assured that it really *is* a grin and not some threatening staring competition; at least, you hope it is! All in all, the Aries cat is a lovable rogue. After it has done all the running around that it can possibly manage, which is generally much more than the average cat, it will gladly come back home to snuggle up on your lap, whether you're ready or not!

Compatibility

Aries human

Two of any Aries, whether they are cats, humans, or one of each, tend not to mesh. When they do, there are sparks, but they can live quite contentedly side by side as long as they try to let each other be exactly who they are.

Taurus human

The Aries cat could be a little wild for the placid Taurus person, rocking the quiet calm a little too often. However, as long as the Aries cat is let out frequently, a good understanding could grow very well between them.

Gemini human

Hang around the Aries feline too often and the Gemini human may start to think and behave exactly like the cat! These two make a happy and lively team, but they'll need to be more considerate of the neighbors.

Cancer human

A disgruntled-looking Aries cat will be a common sight with this duo because the Cancer person will want to ensure that their "coochie-coochie" little cutie cat is always cozy and warm—not something Aries either needs or wants.

Leo human

They feel comfortable together. An Aries cat feels so at home with the Leo person that it will probably start thinking that it's a human being. The Leo human is well in control of this cat, and there's plenty of mutual respect and admiration.

Virgo human

The Virgo person will fuss around the Aries cat every time it throws a bit of litter out of its tray. The Aries cat might just decide to spread a little more around the place simply to watch the Virgo human go ape over a small mess.

Libra human

These two get on brilliantly. There's a distinct and positive love between them. A sense of belonging, of comfort and even a little reflection and projection will naturally develop between these two. They definitely belong together.

Scorpio human

As long as the Scorpio person doesn't try to punish the Aries cat for making small mistakes—for example, stealing just that one sausage left on a plate on the kitchen counter—these two could learn to develop trust.

Sagittarius human

The joint is jumping! The household with a Sagittarius person and an Aries cat living in it is unlikely to be an oasis of calm, but it certainly will be a jungle of action and excitement for those who seek the thrill of non stop bustle.

Capricorn human

Let me out of here! The Aries kitty might feel a little cramped in the Capricorn person's home, even if it's a castle. That's because Capricorn has a way of laying down rules and confinements that rub Aries up the wrong way. There's plenty of outdoor space, though.

Aquarius human

Somehow the Aries cat manages to stay in line around an Aquarius owner. There's mutual reverence and they aim to please one another. No games, no fuss, just rational existence. It makes sense.

Pisces human

This is a no-contest scenario. Frankly, an Aries feline will walk all over the Pisces person. Pisces doesn't have the heart to say "No" to the forthright Aries feline. Anyway, they'll both love it—it's just the way things naturally happen between them.

Taurus | 20 April to 20 May

Taurus | The Supporter

Taurus

Suggested names for the Taurus cat

Moneypenny, Fumbles, Hereford, Hank, Larry, Flubber, Louis, Henry, Tiffany, Dior

Famous cat most likely to have been Taurus

Tom (from Tom & Jerry)

Tenacious

Reliable

Dependable

Laidback

Home-loving

The Taurus cat cat may be laidback and easygoing, but actually it's not the easiest creature to please. That's because this feline likes only the best of everything. Luxury-loving and highly affectionate, it is one of the most beautiful creatures to look at, stroke and appreciate. In addition, it seems to know naturally the value of its surroundings. All felines have a rather aloof manner—that's just a cat's normal demeanor—but a Taurus kitty is expressive. It will do its best to let you know that it loves you and appreciates the expensive, top-quality basket you have kindly provided. It will show its pleasure by rubbing up against your shins and purring at your ankles.

Of all the cats you'll meet, this is the one most likely to prefer the practical things you buy for it. It's just not very excited about fancy toys. It will bat them around once or twice but tends to lose interest in them after it has grown up and put aside kittenish ways, so it's probably not worth wasting the money. This sensual feline does love to be stroked and brushed, however—it just can't get enough of it. It seems to believe that its whole reason for being alive is to enjoy regular physical contact with its owner. This gives it a sense of purpose and security. Therefore, the most important thing to buy for your Taurus cat is a proper brush—one that lightly scratches its coat while you're brushing it.

When you first bring a Taurus kitten or cat into its new home, it may do quite a lot of sitting and looking around—at you, out of the window, at the television. If you try to engage it in play, it'll happily go along with it for a while because it thinks the game is for your benefit, and it would rather make you happy than not. The Taurus cat is a considerate cat, after all. However, it's really not bothered—if you would prefer to go about your usual human business, it will easily fit in with your lifestyle. Once it's settled and knows the score, this down-to-earth cat soon becomes such a permanent fixture in your home and life, that you'll wonder how you ever lived without such a cozy companion. It's truly one of the most loyal and obedient cats, but also not very adaptable. If you try to get it to change its routine—by moving its litter box, for example—you might have a difficult and messy time as a consequence.

As it's such a creature of habit, a Taurus cat generally doesn't like to be moved. Attempt to pick it up from a favored resting place on the most comfortable armchair in the house, and your Taurus moggy seems to gain a hundred pounds right then and there. Loud noises, clapping, and shooing barely manage to raise a whisker. A huge amount of force needs to be exerted to resist it flowing out of your hands and sinking back into its original position. Most people find it easier to sit somewhere else than try to match their Taurus cat for determination and stubbornness.

Similarly, it won't like to venture too far from home. As it is not blessed with a great sense of direction, it would find it highly distressing to get lost and have to cope with strange places and smells. If you ever have to move house, it would be a good idea to keep your Taurus cat indoors for a while, giving it time to get used to its new environment.

When it comes to food, forget the dry stuff, unless it's for a game of "pick and flick." If you happen to have a personal chef, all the better; the Taurus cat is a bit of a connoisseur of haute cuisine, but hey, if there's nothing else, it will eat simply because it likes to eat. In fact, there is a danger of this cat doing nothing else but eating! It's the one area of life where it shakes off its reputation for being unadventurous. The Taurus cat enjoys experimenting with new types of food, so everything from avocado pears to *linguine alle vongole* could make it onto the menu of its favorite dishes. It's also the one thing that makes this somewhat lazy cat react with lightning-quick reflexes. Pause for just a moment with a forkful of food suspended mid-air between plate and mouth, and the Taurus cat will have it off your fork and inside its stomach before you can blink with astonishment!

It's prone to being overweight, so it needs to be encouraged to go outside and have a game. Regular exercise is the only way to get this cat to shift the spare tire that's so typical of this sign. Well, good luck with that! The Taurus cat will enjoy watching people of any age having fun. Actually, that's its favorite game—watching. When it's not exercising its eyeballs or its jaws, it'll happily find a cozy little corner of your yard where it can snooze and take in the beautiful fresh scent of flowers, or just the earth.

Anyway, if you'd wanted a four-legged friend that brought you endless hours of exhausting excitement racing around after it, then you'd have got yourself a terrier, right? Instead, you chose the comforting, affectionate, and oh-so-laidback Taurus cat, which is just the kind of pal you'll want to snuggle up next to on the sofa with a bar of chocolate and a good weepy on the television. By the way, you just might want to hide that chocolate bar under a cushion.

Compatibility

Aries human

These two rub along together quite nicely, though it may not be the closest relationship, as the Aries person may not have the patience to hang around waiting for the Taurus cat to do something exciting, like yawn.

Taurus human

A very companionable match. These two will have lots of cozy times together. And since the Taurus human also goes in for gourmet dining out, the Taurus cat will be in gastronomic heaven with the regular kitty-bags brought home from the best restaurants in town.

Gemini human

Surprisingly, the Taurus cat may be just what a Gemini person needs! Its devotion and loving physical presence is so calming that it provides a therapeutic balm for the frenzied pace of a Gemini's life.

Cancer human

There'll be plenty of home comforts in this household. Not the best cat to have around if the Cancer person is trying to shed a few pounds, as these two will encourage each other to spend hours on the sofa doing nothing but indulging their passion for sweets.

Leo human

This is a pretty good relationship, because the Leo person loves to be loved, adored, and admired—all duties performed perfectly by the loyal Taurus cat. There may be fights over who gets first dibs on the comfy chair, though.

Virgo human

This relationship is fine when they're spending time together in the garden, but as the Taurus cat spends most of its time lazing about the house, the constant cat-hair problem may drive the Virgo person crazy.

Libra human

It's quite probable that the Taurus cat isn't dynamic enough to capture the attention of a Libra human, and the Libra human just won't be as physically affectionate as the Taurus cat needs. But one thing they have in common is appreciation for the finer things in life.

Scorpio human

The Taurus cat will get a lot of care and understanding from its Scorpio human and vice versa, but if it ever does something wrong, then it'll need all its feline independence to cope until it gets back in Scorpio's good books.

Sagittarius human

At least one thing can be said in favor of this relationship and that is that only a Taurus cat would have the amount of patience necessary to wait around for a wayward Sagittarian to come home.

Capricorn human

These two are really on the same wave-length and rarely get in each other's way, but when they do it will be totally fine as they touch base with a scratch behind the ear here, or a purr around the legs there.

Aquarius human

This is not brilliant, but not completely dull either. The Aquarius human is as independent as any feline so they kind of get where the other is coming from. There's unlikely to be a strong intellectual or physical bond, though.

Pisces human

A dreamy combination! Lovely, just what a cat/human relationship should be all about. When the Pisces person wants to sit around getting lost in a daydream, the Taurus cat will curl up on his or her lap, providing an unobtrusive, gentle connection with reality.

Gemini | 21 May to 21 June

Gemini | The Trickster

Gemini

Suggested names for the Gemini cat

Mittens, Icarus, Heckle, Data, Gemini, Licky, Tickles, Teaser, Trixie, Felix, Jekyll and Hyde

Famous cat most likely to have been Gemini

Felix

Curious

Mischievous

Clever

Lively

Funny

The Gemini cat is endlessly busy and easily bored, and what's more, there's seemingly no end to its curiosity. This feline will insist on making friends with all your neighbors and their pets—whether they want to or not. It's a thoroughgoing little busybody, and just wants to poke its nose around every doorway to find out what's going on. You can be sure that if it smells something happening, it'll be the first on the scene! If you don't happen to have neighbors near by, it'll be just as happy to hang around the home keeping you busy shooing it out of your cupboards—the ones where you keep all those yummy treats. Oddly enough, although it's always interested in other people's affairs, at the same time it remains highly independent.

Remember what curiosity did to the cat? Not this one! It's a curious critter all right, but it's also smart, agile, and can be terribly tricky. So yes, it may often get itself into trouble, but just as easily it'll extricate itself in a flash.

If you happen to see a trail of irritated people or pets heading rapidly up the path toward your door, it won't surprise you to learn that one neighbor has had a stack of boxes or a neat row of pot plants knocked over a moment ago, or that one dog was sleeping peacefully until your little friend decided to wake him up to see if he wanted to play a game of chase.

You'll just have to get used to explaining away your pussycat's playful antics by saying that Gemini didn't mean any harm—it never really does—it's just being curious.

It likes heights. Whether it's being chased or looking for a different viewpoint, the Gemini cat's favorite place is up a tree, and the more fiercely it's being chased, the

27

higher up that tree it goes. Vertigo is not something that happens to the Gemini cat; it simply loves being high up in the sky. Its favorite game is chase, but unlike the Aries cat who prefers to be the one doing all the chasing, Gemini is the one that likes to be chased. Chasing becomes an art form. It'll keep the game going for as long as possible, leading its pursuer up hill and down again, only to end up surprising it by turning up behind it—a very tricky cat indeed. Such a tease!

What about mealtimes? Food is not a problem, really. The Gemini cat isn't all that fussy about what you put into its bowl. It'll have dry, moist, or even soggy food, as long as it's tasty and there's plenty of variety. This is not the kind of moggy that gulps down its food all in one go. It much prefers to keep a little in reserve, so that it can come back and snack at intervals throughout the day. The only exception is when it shares its home with a Taurus or a Cancer cat. Then it soon learns that if it doesn't eat fast, it doesn't eat at all. It's a matter of survival!

Gemini is usually pretty slim—all that dashing around interfering in other people's business keeps it lean. So you may be flummoxed when you encounter a little problem. It's something to watch out for with the Gemini cat when it comes to eating habits: your kitty might start gaining weight for no reason that you can imagine. You know that this is a very active and lively cat, and you aren't overfeeding it, so what's going on? This is a sure sign that your freewheeling Gemini cat is leading a double life. The two-timing little devil! The symbol for this sign is the Twins, remember, so don't be too hard on it. Just keep it indoors for a couple of weeks and start watching the local lamp posts for 'Missing' posters featuring a photo or description of your devoted kitty. You may not be able to do much about it, as you have to be pretty cunning to outsmart a Gemini cat. You could come to some agreement over a feeding schedule with the gullible neighbors who have been hoodwinked into thinking that Gemini is their cat, but this could backfire and the last thing you want to do is get into a bidding war about who offers the tastiest food.

Sleeping? What's that? Gemini cats are very light sleepers, which is why yours might be a great night-watchcat! It delicately skips—Gemini cats don't prowl—about the house. It's a wonder that it gets any sleep at all! Even when tiredness overcomes it and it does sleep, it will be with only one eye closed so as to keep the other open and alert to what else might be happening. This cat won't want to miss out on one moment of excitement. But if you're looking for loads of tender, loving cuddles, don't attach yourself to one born under this sign. A Gemini cat is not overly affectionate. This is a thinking feline, and it simply doesn't appear to have the same emotional needs that other more devoted cats have. But that doesn't mean that it doesn't love being in the company of its favorite humans; it's just that it likes to be constantly amused.

A Gemini cat is happiest when it can make you do silly things, like tripping over it, or falling out of bed in fright when it comes pouncing in to wake you up in the morning. This playful pest is the Peter Pan of pussies—it never grows up and will have you giggling with delight or tearing your hair out with frustration. On the other hand, you won't be bored and its amazing personality goes a long way to ensuring it a place in your heart.

Compatibility

Aries human

The Aries person really adores the Gemini cat. These two not only get along, they're positively good for one another especially when one of them has gone out and had a bad day! They'll enjoy being at home and making each other laugh and smile.

Taurus human

This is a relationship that can work. They're like chalk and cheese but they can learn from one another and won't get in each other's way. There's enough similarity to make a good love grow between them.

Gemini human

There's a lot of room for inspiration and a whole heap of creative conversation between these two. They may be talking about two completely different subjects but when these two start chatting, they don't stop.

Cancer human

The Cancer person is the care giver and Gemini cat is the taker. It's pretty straightforward and both parties are willing participants in a pleasant and workable cat/human relationship. It's a good deal for both of them.

Leo human

"We are amused," says the Leo person! These two really love each other's company. No one could come between them, not even a partner of one or the other! There's a feeling of genuine joy between them.

Virgo human

They make a really great team. Busy, busy, busy! There's never a dull moment in a household with a Gemini cat and a Virgo person living together. Although they may not always agree, eventful, engaging, and interesting it will be.

Libra human
There will be no misbehaving between the Libra person and Gemini cat; just lots of enjoyable evenings spent knowing that they completely get each other's thoughts, needs, and desires. A balanced partnership.

Scorpio human
The Gemini kitty might sometimes be forced into submission by the Scorpio owner who has a rigid code of expectations that doesn't include climbing up the curtains just for the fun of it. Gemini will adapt.

Sagittarius human
They're like a see-saw; up one minute and down the next, and yet they'll thrive on one another's company. The Sagittarius person might occasionally complain about the Gemini cat, but actually wouldn't be without it.

Capricorn human
The Capricorn person will eventually catch onto the fact that this kitten will not emotionally mature into a sedate cat as expected. And the Gemini cat will just learn to pussyfoot around the sometimes cranky Capricorn human.

Aquarius human
Is talking to cats allowed? It is if you're an Aquarius person. And is listening part of a Gemini's agenda? Only when it's a cat! These two will get on like cat and cat, or Aquarius and Aquarius—very well indeed.

Pisces human
The clever little Gemini cat might slink around with the confident belief that it has duped that silly human; but it will constantly discover that Pisces was one step ahead and the tin of tuna is no longer where it was!

Cancer

Suggested names for the Cancer cat

Eggroll, Muffin, Babe, Dumpling, Nala, Mango, Macaroni, Nestle, Kushi, Lunatic, Opal, Limpet

Famous cat most likely to have been Cancer

Duchess

Caring

Intuitive

Loving

Protective

Moody

The Cancer cat simply adores food. "Who's the cat that got the cream?" you may well ask. There's no competition—it's just got to be that Cancer kitty. Actually, foods with a high lactose content are not at all the best choice for cats. It's just that the Cancer feline has a passionate liking for its own kind of comfort snack. It may be a bowl of ice cream, or your mom's very own special homemade brownies.

The Cancer cat is in its element when it's curled up on a sofa with you; each of you should be provided with a large serving of your favorite chow! Eating and affection go paw in paw with the Cancer cat, but if you're someone who feels strongly about eating all meals at the dining room table, then be prepared to have a fight on your hands. Your Cancer cat will certainly jump up on the table and generally make a fuss around your ankles at mealtimes.

Eating is the one activity that seems to trigger completely incorrigible habits in your Cancer puss. That's because it believes that sharing your food is the most direct and complete way to make it feel secure. Whoever feeds it will be its favorite person, but not exclusively. This is a pretty affectionate little kitty anyway.

It's important to make sure that any sessions of cozy, loved-up, mutual snacking are scheduled to happen after it has eaten its regular food. That's because it would be typical of this cat to fill up on junk and then not bother with its dinner. By the time the next meal comes around, it'll demand something fresh, not the stuff that has been sitting there since snack time.

It's always easy to recognize a contented Cancer cat by the distinctively spherical-shaped belly it develops, looking for all the world as though it has just swallowed the

35

Moon, the celestial object that rules this sign. This cat also loves its home—fiercely. In fact, it's probably more territorial than most cats. Rarely venturing outside the yard in case there are frightening monsters out there ready to gobble it up, the Cancer cat plays the part of the prowling sentinel. It orbits its home on the look out for invaders and ready to raise the alarm by dashing to your side the moment strangers approach. "Fraidy cat? Moi?"

In fact, everyone is welcome to come in as long as it approves; you'll be glad to know that this includes most human beings, but hardly any other animals! Just watch its little face fall if you treat some other person's pet as though it were your own pretty baby. How could you do that? Cancer cat will get into a terrible mood over such an outrage! Visiting humans who don't like cats will be the first to receive its affectionate attention. It instinctively senses someone's silent aversion, and will have an irresistible urge to overcome that aversion with love. The Cancer cat is incredibly sensitive to the moods of others, and quite determined to give its affection where and when it feels there is the most need for it, regardless of how welcome that affection is. Could this be a clever ploy to gain another companion to snack with? Don't be so cynical! This cat is really quite spooky in the way that it intuits the undercurrents of the emotional atmosphere. If ever there was a cat suited to being the familiar of a witch-in-training, then the Cancer cat must be first in line. Protecting and nurturing the more vulnerable aspects of its human's emotions and spirit comes quite naturally.

Trust the Cancer cat to find its own sleeping place—it'll probably be in a pile of blankets or towels in the linen closet, otherwise it very much enjoys having its own comfy, cozy basket, a home within a home. It'll prefer it to be filled with cushions and anything soft that makes it feel coddled. However, you may have to put on a pair of rubber gloves and have a regular poke around in its basket when it's not looking. That's because Cancer kitties are known as keen collectors of mementos to which they become sentimentally attached. They will accumulate quite a treasure trove, including some smelly objects.

The favorite games of the Cancer cat are played outdoors—they are the ones where it can prowl around the yard on its belly, watching other animals, and getting ready to pounce. You can easily imagine that it's thinking just how tasty those birds and squirrels would be, if only it could catch them! It will try, of course, but it's not as successful as the faster and more agile cats hunting out there in the wild. That's precisely why it tends to treat any successful catch as a trophy; it boosts its sense of self-esteem to keep a constant reminder of its prowess in the skills of survival.

If you're worried about your home getting messy, this is an easy cat to house train—it's the feline equivalent of a domestic goddess (or god.) It'll have a few ideas of its own about how a household should be run. It might drag its litter box somewhere that it thinks is more convenient. The Cancer cat has the ability to initiate, and uses it well.

This kitty is the essential ingredient to turn your house, apartment or trailer into a real home. Its constant, loving support makes it indispensable to your sense of wellbeing, because when you've got a Cancer cat, you know you've got a family.

Compatibility

Aries human

The Cancer cat may be a little too needy of constant cozy affection for the typical Aries person who is always dashing around. It might be better to get a cat that is more independent and won't try to hang off you as you walk out the door.

Taurus human

Now this is just the right person to appreciate all the wonderful, loving qualities of the Cancer cat, though both will have to watch their waistlines as they spend all those hours snuggling up on the sofa indulging in delicious treats.

Gemini human

Most of the time the Gemini person really enjoys being with a Cancer cat. But Gemini folk can easily get very caught up in their own thinking, and may not even notice that kitty has moved in with that nice Taurus person down the road.

Cancer human

These two will be in touch on an intuitive as well as an emotional level—they'll always know where the other is and when they'll be home. It will depend on the particular occasion as to which one is at the front door to provide the welcome.

Leo human

The Cancer cat will be spoilt rotten by the generous Leo person which, as far as the puss is concerned, is just purrfect. But Leos should be warned that this kind of indulgence will mean that the Cancer cat will never leave them alone for a minute.

Virgo human

Most of the house rules and routines set down by the Virgo person will suit the Cancer cat very well, but it just won't understand that snuggling up on the sofa is not as attractive to the Virgo as it is to them. What's wrong with a few cat hairs?

Libra human

Libra likes company, but would really prefer a feline that is somewhat more mentally curious and physically active than the typical cozy Cancer kitty. This relationship works best if the home they share has a large walled garden.

Scorpio human

The Cancer cat will be more fascinated with the Scorpio person than with any other, and will feel totally secure and comfortable with a human companion as emotionally intuitive and territorial as itself.

Sagittarius human

The Cancer cat will love being around a Sagittarius! However, the problem is that Sagittarius isn't around that often, which means that there had better be some other people in the home to hang out with. Otherwise Cancer cat will be insecure and lonely.

Capricorn human

This isn't a bad combination, but on the other hand, it's not great either. The Capricorn person is very responsible and will see to all the Cancer cat's physical needs well enough, but those cozy, comfy bonding sessions will be very few on the ground.

Aquarius human

Although this person will enjoy the attention and affection offered by the Cancer cat, Aquarius is tuned to a different psychic frequency most of the time, leaving the Cancer cat having to find other, more noisy ways to communicate.

Pisces human

A lovely bond can develop between these two. Pisces' natural empathy for the emotional needs of the Cancer cat will ensure that every one of these will be met without it even having to say "Meow!"

Leo | 23 July to 23 August

Suggested names for the Leo cat

Caesar, Leo, Fluffy, Lucky, Napoleon, Rex, Tsarina, Dandy, Brummel, Goldy, Sunshine, Glamorpuss

Famous cat most likely to have been Leo

Top Cat

Regal

Enthusiastic

Energetic

Loyal

Charismatic

The Leo cat is a very happy cat indeed. It's extremely happy in its own fur; and doesn't have the same complex that some felines get, like thinking it's a human disguised as a cat. It loves itself just as it is, proud of its elegant form and simply delighted to take every opportunity to strut around giving its human admirers a chance to worship it. It has such a bright, sunny personality because, to its way of thinking, "Everybody Wants To Be a Cat!" Although all kittens enjoy a good play fight, the Leo kitten goes in for a serious game of Conquers. It loves the rough and tumble and the excitement of challenge. What's more, it is always in there right to the end, because its skills are superior—kingly, you might say. Giving up before the prize has been won would never enter its little head. This baby lion grows up to become confident and strong, yet gentle and loving at the same time. It simply adores being stroked—you'll just have to remember that, because your Leo cat will never demean itself to come begging for what it wants. Give freely to it and it'll behave like a little prince or princess: impeccably.

That said, it's also true that the regal Leo feline is perhaps the most pompous of all the cats. Just watch for a while—it really does walk around with its nose in the air, and it expects to be pampered and served at all times. You won't catch a Leo cat behaving like some common moggy, screeching to be fed or making a fuss at mealtimes. It'll simply sit majestically by its bowl, tail curled stylishly around its paws. Meanwhile, its eyes will bore holes in the back of your head until you have laid out its meal. There's also a tendency for it to be somewhat dismissive of its owners, and you might start to feel a bit like a court jester in your attempts to get this kitty's attention. This is something you should be particularly aware of when it comes to training. And that's why it's very important to begin instruction at the earliest possible moment. Good habits start young, and Leo cats very quickly become set in their ways.

Your little Leo may be majestic and proud, but surprisingly, it's not as demanding as you might think. Because of its superior attitude and the lofty way it carries itself, you'd be forgiven for projecting some of your own thoughts about what it would like. But in fact,it doesn't need a lot of frills—this is a naturally noble creature. Its basket doesn't have to be a fancy gold-plated throne, though it certainly wouldn't pass it up if one was on offer. Also, it will do its absolute best to present an impressive tableau to show itself

off should any guests drop around for a visit—a Leo cat would never let the side down when it comes to keeping up appearances. Mostly, however, it just needs something supremely comfortable, and something of long lasting, durable quality—it knows what it likes, so you might have to try out a few before it settles on one.

The Leo cat is a hunter by nature and likes its meat fresh and preferably dripping with gore. You may choose to feed it on dried food, but the moment you let it out of your sight, it'll be scrounging around outside your neighbors' trash can sniffing out leftover bones, or perhaps scaling tree trunks in search of a bird.

Generosity is a Leo's middle name, and these lovely cats are no exception. Let your Leo outdoors and it'll big-heartedly bring back a gift for you clutched in its jaws. It also does this to show off its prowess in the wild, and since it recognizes your inability to do the same, it's really just trying to help. Whatever private feelings you have about being presented with a wriggling food offering, be sure to praise your Leo cat for these displays of skill and generosity. Although it is unlikely to acknowledge your eager gratitude publicly, its ego is particularly delicate and it would be devastated if its gift wasn't received with some kind of fanfare.

Indeed, it is the one true need of these otherwise highly self-sufficient individuals. Being admired, adored, and appreciated for the stylish superstar it knows itself to be is crucial to its sense of security and self-confidence. It can get a little wearing, constantly having to massage the ego of a Leo cat, particularly as it expects to hear applause every time it deigns to walk into a room, but you'll soon see that it's worth the effort. A pedigree Leo make an excellent show cat, as it loves playing to an audience. It may also turn out to be something of a gold mine for you as the sire or queen of other famous champions. But even a crossbred Leo mog could give other purebred cats a run for their money when it comes to showing off the graceful and elegant lines of the feline form.

The older Leo feline prefers to spend its time stretched out in a lazy sprawl doing absolutely nothing! Most cats choose a shady spot under the bushes or a safe corner of the kitchen. Not your Leo. Smack bang in the middle of the path, doorway, or floor is its preferred position, right where people have to step over or walk around it. It may no longer feel the need to show off quite so much, but being relegated to the realms of unseen obscurity? Never!

Compatibility

Aries human

This is a great friendship. Aries gives Leo the exact dose of love, respect, and adoration it needs without being smothering or patronizing. The Leo cat will rest and play in perfect rhythm with the lively Aries household. They'll both get what they need.

Taurus human

The Leo kitty's needs are wildly extravagant, which is just what the Taurus person can satisfy. However, it must all be on the Taurus human's terms, which could frustrate this small lion. A lot of outdoor action is the perfect remedy.

Gemini human

Gemini is footloose and fancy free—just what the Leo cat loves in a human. It's all action around this household and they'll both love the way they have to dance around one another with all the commotion.

Cancer human

A peaceful, loving partnership. The Cancer person has a calming influence on the Leo cat, so together they'll get along like peaches and cream—perfectly coordinated, with plenty of sweet moments that go down very smoothly for both.

Leo human

In a very light-hearted way, these two will be competing to find out who's boss! One day the Leo person will want to put his or her foot down and not allow another treat, and the next it'll be kitty getting it all for free.

Virgo human

A classic master-servant relationship. It might seem as if the Virgo person waits on this big cat hand and foot, and that wouldn't be too far from the truth. There's always something for the dutiful Virgo human to do for the regal Leo cat.

Libra human

This is a pleasant partnership because neither will be too fussed about the demands of the other. The Leo cat will naturally behave and knows its place, while the Libra person just loves having such a gorgeous cat to show off.

Scorpio human

Day by day, there will be more than one tense moment in the life of Leo cat and Scorpio person. There's always something that seems to cause mutual annoyance, but naturally, the Scorpio person will win because size matters here.

Sagittarius human

If cats could be heard when they laugh, then the Leo cat would constantly be smiling and chuckling, not at its Sagittarian owner but definitely with him or her! Watch out, this could turn into a rip-roaring, raucous household.

Capricorn human

The Leo cat could become a tad snide around Capricorn; it stares at this owner in disbelief while thinking things like "Is that all?" and "You want me to eat that?" Capricorn's lifestyle is a little spartan for this poor little rich kitty.

Aquarius human

Love, love me do! There *is* a kind of love affair going on between these two! In fact, when the Aquarius human is snuggling up with a lover, the Leo cat will want to mark its territory by sitting on its owner's lap, and refusing to move.

Pisces human

The Leo cat will get away with a lot with the Pisces person. That's perfectly all right with Pisces, but this lax attitude could annoy the Leo cat so it's more likely to spend time outdoors where the boundaries are firm—it needs them.

Suggested names for the Virgo cat

Calico, Sparkle, Mopsy, Morris, Patch, Sadie (the cleaning lady), Sweep, Tweenie, Prissy

Famous cat most likely to have been Virgo

Snagglepuss

Meticulous

Intelligent

Calm

Practical

Modest

The Virgo cat seems to spend significantly more time grooming, preening, and cleaning than most other cats. It's true that all cats clean themselves regularly—the licking of fur is thought to help keep them warm by adding another layer of insulation. It also helps them to stay cool on hot days by keeping the fur moist. Cats also like to get rid of the scents that people leave when stroking them. Each one prefers to maintain its own signature smell by licking its coat. It usually does this in a particular order.

So, we've established that all cats like to be clean, but the Virgo cat will take this process far more seriously than others. It's much fussier and tidier, which is all very fine unless your own level of hygiene doesn't match its standards! Be warned. It will go on hunger strike if its bowls are not kept meticulously spotless, and it won't be putting its precious little paws in an overflowing litter box! So, if you want your Virgo kitty to be happy and calm, you must keep everything scrupulously clean.

Of course it will eat what you put in front of it, but the Virgo cat would prefer to eat food that's recognizable for what it is rather than the shaped variety that contains all that artificial flavoring and additives. If it had the choice, it would have only the purest, freshest ingredients. If you could cook up a nice dish of bite-size meat and vegetables in a small amount of gravy and serve it up warm (not hot), you'd have one truly satisfied kitty. It would be quite easy to make a larger amount than you need, freeze it into meal-size food bags, and defrost one at a time. Efficiency is the Virgo cat's middle name and you'll soon find yourself picking up its habits. It has excellent table manners and is extremely prompt at mealtimes. You can set your watch by your Virgo cat; it will suddenly appear in the kitchen out of nowhere at the usual and correct time. So shape up: if you are not fully prepared, ready and waiting to serve its meal, you'll certainly hear about it, as the Virgo cat can get quite vocal in its criticism of your sloppy time-keeping.

When young, the Virgo kitten will play like any kitty does; it's fast, agile, and very light on its feet, but it's more drawn by games with a "now-you-see-it-now-you-don't" theme. It'll sweetly fall for the disappearing ball or string trick every time and try to find out where it has gone. Nothing is quite as cute as the Virgo kitten tipping its little head from side to side, as it sits wide-eyed and alert pondering the problem of catching that plaything. As it grows, this will amuse it less and less, and

instead it will prefer to spend its time surveying its territory or engaged in its favorite pastime—you guessed it—cleaning itself.

It must be said that, thanks to its fleetfooted agility and analytical brain, the Virgo cat is extremely clever at working out the purpose of those puzzling domestic gadgets. Door handles are usually the first things that this bright spark will want to decipher. It'll soon work out that jumping up onto the bureau and then launching itself at the handle with outstretched paws, twisting just in time to land dextrously on all fours, will open the door. This allows it to get out of any room where it has been accidentally shut in so that it can make it to the litter box should the need arise. Being unable to do so could make a Virgo cat extremely neurotic. That's not just because it's so fastidious in its habits that it would be mortified if forced to use a pot plant. It's also that not being able to solve a problem that humans have no difficulty in mastering would make it feel like a very feeble feline indeed. And that would be sad, as the Virgo cat always likes to be helpful. This is a very reasonable cat and it is really not into making a tremendous fuss for no reason. Self-sufficiency, as well as cleanliness, is next to catliness.

The Virgo cat doesn't expect much in the way of sleeping arrangements. It's quite happy to snuggle down in a designated place near the kitchen or have a simple little basket in the spare room. Just remember to keep its space tidy, or it'll start acting fickle by refusing to go anywhere near the spot where it once seemed to be so contented.

Generally the Virgo cat is the ultimate in low-maintenance pets—so much so that it's easy to fall into

the trap of taking it for granted! Except for its demands for a well-organized, clean home and dinner promptly on the dot, it rarely makes a fuss about anything. If, however, your Virgo cat seems a touch peaky, off its food, or not paying very much attention to its personal hygiene, then rush it straight to the veterinary surgery. On such occasions this self-healing cat will have need of rather more sophisticated medical treatment than chewing on a few blades of grass.

Your Virgo feline may not be as playful as a Gemini, as showy as a Leo, or as devoted as a Taurus, but it's a really good friend and a great listener. Tell it about your problems and it'll always be happy to help with a well-timed quizzical tilt of the head if you're talking nonsense. On the other hand, when you've hit on the right solution, it will have a lovely long, approving stretch!

Compatibility

Aries human

This is an easy relationship only because the Virgo cat is so helpful. It knows that causing a fuss could result in its Aries human getting irritated, which, given the noise volume attached to that irritation, is best avoided.

Taurus human

The Virgo cat will thrive in the company of a Taurus person—it will appreciate the calm atmosphere and is less likely to become neurotic. However, it will probably head out for more exercise in order to work off the extra calorie intake.

Gemini human

At first these two will have a lot of fun, but eventually the Virgo cat may start to form the opinion that its unpredictable Gemini friend is a bit crazy and will avoid getting directly involved, preferring to watch from a safe distance.

Cancer human

The Virgo cat loves to be needed. Normally it maintains a polite reserve when it comes to intruding on personal space, but it will become cozier and more snuggly with a Cancer owner than with any other.

Leo human

It is unlikely that any person will fascinate the Virgo cat as much as a Leo. It might hang around the house more often so that it can watch the dramas that unfold. Leo humans are more likely to put on a show for such an appreciative audience.

Virgo human

This is a very functional relationship—both will be impressed by and pleased with the hygiene habits of the other. But with two such reserved creatures sharing the same living space, there isn't a lot of potential for a strong emotional bond to develop.

Libra human

Mirror, mirror on the wall…? Most of the time the Virgo cat will be ready to answer this question with a resounding "You are!" But eventually feline conscience will demand that it lets the Libra human know that there are more important things in life.

Scorpio human

The Virgo cat may be just a bit too prim and proper for a Scorpio human who likes to see a bit of oomph and a healthy amount of aggression in their feline companions. This will be friendly but without a deeper bond.

Sagittarius human

Although the Sagittarius person doesn't notice whether things are kept clean and tidy, these two will do very well together provided that, during long absences from home, Sagittarius arranges for someone else to serve meals promptly.

Capricorn human

An excellent arrangement. Both will respect each other's needs and always be reliably uncomplicated when it comes to their relationship. No matter what they face in the outside world, with each other they know exactly where they stand.

Aquarius human

The need to stand up for the undercat is part of the Aquarius person's character. But that may diminish the Virgo cat's self-esteem, simply because every time it is involved in a dispute with another cat, this human jumps in and takes over.

Pisces human

There are loads of things that the Virgo cat will really love about its Pisces pal, but dreadful time-keeping is not one of them! However hard it tries to reform its owner, Virgo puss might as well try to hold back the tides with its tail.

Suggested names for the Libra cat

Adonis, Kashmir, Greta, Gucci, Handel, Astaire, Leonardo, Romeo, Rosaline, Abigail, Ribbons, Zsa Zsa

Famous cat most likely to have been Libra

Puss in Boots

Graceful

Genial

Gentle

Flirtatious

Intelligent

The Libra cat is all sweetness and light—you can almost see it smiling at you. This cat is a consummate schmoozer and it simply loves people. In fact, it can be so inviting and amiable, that it'll rush to answer the door every time it hears the bell ring. Your Libra feline is also beautiful to look at, no matter what breed it is. There's something refined and elegant about the way it carries itself, even as a kitten. This cat is so light on its feet that it often appears to glide across the floor. It can make a jump up onto a table or window ledge look effortless—as if it had simply wished itself there, and gravity had accommodated it by ceasing to exist for a moment. "Graceful" is a word that was specially invented to describe it.

Your Libra puss is desperate without company, however. It will follow you around the house constantly, but as it has impeccable manners, it won't always be jumping into your lap or purring about your ankles. Instead, it'll simply float into a room at your heels and take up a position from where it can observe your activities, only racing to your side when called. This need for companionship may be a tad wearing. You have to go out sometimes, after all—and you may want to take a bath without your friendly cat perched on the edge of the tub watching your every move.

Libra puss will sense your mood and simply head out in search of another companion. It will early on have made friends with the neighbors' cats, a comforting insurance against any moments of loneliness. This isn't a problem if your cat is male; otherwise it could lead to expensive vet's bills from inoculating so many kittens! Observing the way a female Libra cat conducts herself when she's in heat gives a pretty good idea of the ways she entices the male into mating. She emits special scents and makes particularly alluring sounds to let all the males within her vicinity know that she's ready! It's a bit like a passionate Hollywood movie—in fact, the whole process of dating and mating may take several days!

As for suitable sleeping arrangements, your Libra feline, even when it's a male, prefers a bit of satin and lace. If you're not into all that prissy, pretty paraphernalia, then a tartan rug or something with a logical pattern will do just as well: this cat's sharp mind enjoys contemplating symmetry. Just make sure that the bedding is soft and sensuous! Even a little silk cushion will let it know that you're trying to please it because you know it has a taste for the finer things in life. You don't have to go over the top and choose designer names or buy a ruby-encrusted collar, though if you do, your Libra cat won't complain. It'll just slink and sweep even more intently around your feet with its soft, flowing tail whispering along the surface of your skin, making the rounds and nuzzling its face between your feet to let you know how much it appreciates and loves you. This is a clever tactic, and Libra puss knows it, because the next time you go shopping, you'll end up splashing out and coming back with the *pâté de foie gras* without even realizing it. That's right, your luxury-loving pet has been sending you telepathic messages. Charm is one of the most powerful weapons in this cat's arsenal, and boy, does it it wield it like a master!

We all know that cats are renowned for their sense of balance, but the Libra feline has this down to an art form. It has a supremely superior sense of balance. On the rare occasion when it does fall, it always seems to manage to land on its feet—there's an instinctive twisting method to the way a cat will right itself, and it does this in mid-air and in a split second. Incredible, really. Libra is also weighing things up when its eyes are fixed on some prey and it's preparing to pounce—have you noticed the way its head moves from side to side? This is how your cat determines the exact distance and calculates the necessary moves and speed in order to capture its prey.

However, your beloved Libra cat may sometimes spend so much time calculating the odds that it leaves things just that split second too long before making the pounce. Never mind, it doesn't really have an appetite for wild game, it's more the intellectual puzzle of getting the prowl and pounce right that interests this creature.

Libra puss will prefer to eat the way you do, in a designated dining area, and from a clean bowl. In fact, it's something of a copycat. Really, it's so convinced that it's every bit as human as you that it will even try to take the food to its mouth by the delicate use of a paw rather than shoving its face in it. Once again it will demonstrate superior social skills and excellent table manners, because, unless it's really very hungry, it will wait by the food in its bowl and start to eat only once you are seated at the table and beginning your own meal.

The refined and sociable Libra cat is the perfect companion for anybody who needs to be reminded that grace and beauty are virtues of the highest order. It's the perfect cat if you already subscribe to that opinion, because this like-minded feline will soon become your very best and most cherished friend.

Compatibility

Aries human

Like Fire and Air, these two feed off one another and together they make a pretty lovely and lively household. They give each other independence and space, and yet both offer affection and unspoken understanding when they need it.

Taurus human

Both have a sparkle from Venus, and have the kind of sweet love that's bonded by the most tender steak and gravy, plenty of leftover pie and cream followed by a delicate sip of the finest mineral water, or in the case of the human, wine.

Gemini human

The Libra cat loves the light and airy feeling it gets when it's around a Gemini person. There's no fuss and no fight; just food when it needs it, cuddles when it wants them, and a warm place to sleep—bliss!

Cancer human

The Cancer person may not be the perfect companion for the Libra cat, but they'll certainly give one another their best shot. There is mutual respect and the essential needs of both parties will be upheld.

Leo human

The Libra cat will love to live with a Leo person simply because of the high standard of living—first-class food and upholstery. There's quality all round, and that suits the luxury-loving Libra puss.

Virgo human

This is such an attentive owner, with a great eye for that important detail. Libra can do without all the frills when it's being looked after by a Virgo person—after all, Virgo will perfectly take care of all the essential needs of the Libra cat, who will want for nothing at all.

Libra human

Likes attract. These two will think alike. They eat at the same time, sleep at the same time, often even in the same bed. They may even start to look alike, and they might as well, as they're already starting to adopt the same mannerisms!

Scorpio human

The Scorpio person complements the Libra cat fairly well. Their lifestyles can be quite different, as Scorpio is intense while Libra takes it easy, but in that way they click in perfectly to one another's vibe.

Sagittarius human

The Libra cat will love the way Sagittarians live—they're so wild and, well, so beastly! OK, that might sound a bit rich coming from a cat, but Libra is a sophisti-cat. And the Sagittarius person will enjoy this hassle-free feline friend.

Capricorn human

There could be the occasional cold shoulder in both directions, but that won't stop this pair from being drawn toward one another. A useful observation: Capricorn is happier with the Libra cat than the other way round.

Aquarius human

The Libra cat will take more interest in the Aquarius person than Aquarius has time to give back. However, this is just as well, because they'll both enjoy the independence, and yet there's plenty of love to go round.

Pisces human

The Pisces person would be happier with a kitty who gives a little more on the emotional front, and the Libra cat would prefer a more active and dynamic human, but that doesn't mean that they can't provide something for one another.

Scorpio | 23 October to 21 November

scorpio

Suggested names for the Scorpio cat

Sonic, Catty, Diggy, Caligula, Ebony, Fanny, Hiss, Spanky, Lilith, Ninja, Magic, Mysteron, Dalek

Famous cat most likely to have been Scorpio

Sylvester

Passionate

Secretive

Intense

Dedicated

Competitive

The Scorpio cat is the cattiest of cats—you can hear it in its voice! You'll sometimes detect a distinctly sneery tone rather than a merry little "Meow!" Snide and snippy but splendidly savvy, this is one cool cat. You'd have to get up pretty early in the morning to fool it. It knows exactly where to find the best tidbits—in the trash bin. Sadly, it won't be unusual for you to walk into the kitchen in the morning to find garbage strewn all over the floor with no obvious evidence as to how it happened. You should know that the Scorpio cat is naturally sneaky. It is excellent at hiding away to avoid being present at moments like this in case it incriminates itself. And if it does have the temerity to be there at the moment of discovery, it'll sit looking out of the window as if butter wouldn't melt in its mouth. This means, of course, that you won't be able to scold your Scorpio cat because you can only justifiably admonish it for something when you've caught it in the act! And you'll need to spend several sleepless nights in a row if you want to catch it red-pawed.

The Scorpio cat is a bundle of nervous energy, and because of this intensity of feeling it tends to scratch at furniture and upholstery more than other cats. While the Aries cat is very outgoing with its energy, and the Taurus cat tends not to display an enormous amount of extra vim and verve, the Scorpio cat is utterly brimful of vigor. But it is highly idiosyncratic in the way it uses this energy. It will gnaw or scratch incessantly, especially if it's not allowed to go outdoors very often. Every cat needs to scratch of course; and the reason for this is not just to sharpen its claws. It also serves to scrape away a layer of sheath in order to reveal a fresh claw beneath.

It also has the added advantage of allowing the cat to mark its scent, an appealing prospect for the hugely territorial Scorpio feline.

Most importantly, scratching is a way for your cat to exercise its front feet, its main weapons when it comes to catching prey, fighting, and climbing to safety. So scratching is an important natural instinct in every cat and is not an easy habit to break. In the case of the Scorpio cat, it's practically an impossibility.

The solution is to find a way for it to express its instincts safely. You can either provide more outdoor space for it to sharpen those busy claws on old tree stumps and branches or, if you are an upper-story apartment-dweller and want to preserve your furnishings, then most pet stores will be able to sell you a scratching post covered in a coarse material perfect for your Scorpio cat to get its claws into.

The Scorpio cat also has a highly attuned sensory perception. We know that cats can detect a change in the magnetic field just prior to an earthquake, but they are also incredibly intuitive about emotions. Indeed, at one time, cats were punished and killed in the belief that they were witches' familiars, and people would cease a conversation if a cat walked by in case the cat carried any secrets back to its witch-owner. The fact is that cats are capable of picking up vibes that most humans aren't aware of.

You might notice that your puss often seems to be sitting quietly and looking at you the moment you wake up, so you wonder who was there first? Was it you who realized that there was a cat staring at you which made you wake up, or did your supersweet and sentient little Scorpio kitty know that you were just coming out of sleep and decide to greet you good morning? It's a little unnerving at first, perhaps even spooky, but the mysterious Scorpio cat will carry its secrets to the grave, so it looks like you'll have to learn to live with it.

When it comes to its own sleeping habits, the Scorpio cat prefers a secret little hidey-hole for its bed. A basket would be too open and exposed, so even if you buy it the most comfortable and expensive one in the pet store, it probably won't use it. Don't be surprised if it dismisses the basket and instead sleeps at the back of the linen closet where you keep your extra blankets.

A trip to the pet store, where you can pick up a cat bed that resembles a miniature sleeping bag, might be the best solution, unless of course you particularly enjoy the pungent perfume of cat spray permeating all your sheets, towels, and blankets.

When it comes to food your Scorpio cat is partial to fresh, even bloody, meat. It won't complain if it doesn't appear too often on the menu. It's more than happy to wait for some unsuspecting little creature to scurry past or fly down to within pouncing distance. This is both a pleasurable game and a practical way of indulging its occasional yen for superfresh food.

The Scorpio cat won't suddenly become your best friend; even as a kitten it keeps itself under tight control, preferring to spy out the situation first before volunteering any obvious cozy affection. But over time a Scorpio puss is a devoted and loyal cat, linked to its human by some deep emotional and psychic bond. You'll belong to it as much as it to you, so don't ever make it jealous by stroking or talking to some other cat—or you might just need a band-aid.

Compatibility

Aries human

Aries owners may have a bit of a problem coming to terms with the secretive nature of the Scorpio cat as they prefer everything out in the open, but they'll thoroughly understand the need for a scratching post to sharpen its claws on.

Taurus human

The patience of Taurus will be tested to the hilt by seeing precious possessions scratched up and ruined. Taurus also won't appreciate the spoils of the hunt brought in by the Scorpio cat. Yet in every other way they enjoy being together.

Gemini human

These two will never understand each other, even though both have a keen form of intelligence. However, that doesn't mean that this relationship will be a huge disaster; just a string of minor ones dotted in between the good times.

Cancer human

Most of the time this is a really great combination, with both thoroughly in tune on a psychic level. However, when the Scorpio cat displays the more snippy, sneery side of its nature, the sensitive Cancer person's feelings could be hurt.

Leo human

The play fights between these two could escalate rapidly into something more serious, with neither the human nor the cat prepared to back down. Funnily enough, this won't seem to bother either of them. They love it!

Virgo human

Virgo owners will certainly not enjoy the experience of finding nasty pieces of discarded prey hidden around the home, yet they are forgiving enough to realize that this is totally natural behavior in their feline friend.

Libra human

The Libra person should get really well clued up to the needs of the Scorpio cat to retreat inside a cozy hidey-hole. Then there'll be no need to freak out about the Scorpio puss getting territorial over all those lovely designer clothes hanging in the closet.

Scorpio human

An equal partnership. These two admire and understand each other purrfectly. They know instinctively when to back off and give the other some space and when to offer their hand or paw in an emotional display of friendship.

Sagittarius human

The Sagittarius person will be highly impressed by the hunting skills of the Scorpio cat but is not usually around long enough to develop the strong emotional or psychic bond that is possible with this feline.

Capricorn human

There are no problems with this combination—both know where they're at with the other. They carry on their separate lives, perfectly confident that any time they require some more attention, they only have to meow, or ask.

Aquarius human

The way a Scorpio cat taunts and plays with its prey may disturb the humanitarian sensibilities of Aquarians, but that's their problem! After all, it's a cat they've chosen to share their home with! Once they realize that, it's fine.

Pisces human

Spooky! It is difficult to know which one of them is the spookiest. The Pisces person is wise at once to all the secretive tactics employed by the Scorpio cat, just as the cat can sense exactly when this human is heading its way.

Sagittarius | 22 November to 21 December

sagittarius

Suggested names for the Sagittarius cat

Liberty, Gypsy, Bali, Abbey, Dallas, Katmandu, Hunter, Olympus, Plato, Soda, Rover, Lofty, Joy

Famous cat most likely to have been Sagittarius

Cat in the Hat

Adventurous

Optimistic

Enthusiastic

Jolly

Happy-go-lucky

Sagittarius is the wild cat of the bunch! Rambunctious and energetic, it really does love to play. This is not the kind of cat to be kept indoors—if you try to keep it in because of your home setup, then it will find its way out. Harry Houdini was probably a Sagittarius cat in a previous life! Once it has escaped, don't expect it to rush back indoors—given the taste of freedom and the great outdoors, this cat will want some time to explore. In fact, it seems to disappear for an extraordinary and frighteningly long time. The truth is that it needs lots of space to wander; a Sagittarius cat is a true freedom lover, and just cannot be tied down, cooped up, or held back. Although this can be a worry for you, there's rarely any need: it never really gets lost because it has such a great sense of direction, but the bigger its personal space, the better it likes it.

The world belongs to the adventurous Sagittarius cat; it simply can't get enough of it, so it just keeps on trekking, exploring, and experiencing. After all, a cat's territory can stretch over one hundred acres, especially if it's a farm cat. Occasionally, after a particularly grueling escapade, it might return with the telltale signs that it has wandered too far into the territory of some larger animal, like a raccoon or a fox; sometimes its wounds will require an immediate visit to the veterinary surgery. You'll naturally be terribly worried and upset, but really the Sagittarius cat is a hardy animal, and if it could talk, the stories it would tell would definitely make every adventure worth while. Part of the reason why this feline has a habit of getting into these entanglements in the first place is that it dares to go beyond the parameters—it pushes limits and

Sagittarius | The Playmate

expectations. But the main reason for getting into skirmishes is that it appears so full of bravado that it naturally attracts unwelcome attention from larger creatures.

Most cats will, at some time, hunch their backs up and flare out their fur when trying to protect themselves against a possible threat. However, the Sagittarius cat probably does this a little more often than other cats in an attempt to look larger than it really is! The whole purpose of hunching and flaring is, hopefully, to make it possible for it to frighten off any large beasts. It's just that a Sagittarius cat enjoys this sort of exaggeration a whisker too much. Consequently, it's bound to get twice as many challenges as the average puss.

Actually, the Sagittarius cat is not always on the go; it needs its moments of rest and recuperation, and when it's at home it really does

love to stretch out and relax. Have you ever seen a cat dozing flat on its back, front and back legs spread-eagled, soft furry underbelly exposed to the world? That was probably a Sagittarius cat, because even when resting it has to take up as much space as possible. In its quieter moments this cat can spend hours sitting on a window ledge watching the world go by and contemplating its next adventure, studying the people and other animals it sees. It will be so lost in its thoughts that several noisy children could come bounding into the room and the Sagittarius cat would not even twitch an ear.

It becomes so comfortable in its surroundings and yours that it also feels free to share absolutely everything. Your bed is its favorite place to sleep, which makes sense—you keep it warm, it's always clean, it's soft and cozy, and best of all it can snuggle up to you! It would never occur to a Sagittarius puss that it might be unwelcome, or that it was somehow in your way; it has a naturally optimistic expectation that you want exactly what it wants.

If you have decided to share your home with a Sagittarius cat don't expect it to be polite and well mannered—it will bring the spoils of its hunt inside to plop right on top of your expensive Persian rug. Then it'll spend the next half-hour playing with the corpse, tossing it around, and catching it again as if trying to encourage it to behave the way it did when it was still alive and more fun. The Sagittarius cat loves to hunt, and spends most of its time either doing just that or practicing for the time when the game is afoot. It also prefers to stay in peak physical condition, so acrobatic backflips off the sofa and endless athletic sprints around the house will be regular

sporting activities. It seems to be particularly fond of doing this at night, just after all has gone quiet, the lights are out, and you are drifting off to sleep. You'll be glad to know that your Sagittarius cat is just practicing night-vision maneuvers.

There's no doubt about it: the Sagittarius cat is a regular slob when it comes to eating—well, compared to most other cats, anyway. It'll chow down on anything, and usually makes a mess by playing with its food, pushing its bowls around the floor, or flipping it around in order to make it seem as if it's catching live prey. Once the game's over and it has eaten everything, your cat will bolt out of the kitchen and leave any fallout for you to clean up. The messy tyke! But oh, it's so much more fun than other people's tame kitties—and it's such a brave and fascinating creature! How could you possibly resist a Sagittarius moggy?

Compatibility

Aries human

A match made in heaven, as they are the original dynamic duo! It would be a surprise if their home didn't start to look tattered and torn within the first six months of living together, but they will be happy and will never tire of one another.

Taurus human

These two are unlikely to have a lot in common, but they'll tolerate one another for want of better company. The Taurus person will certainly provide for the Sagittarius cat, but Sagittarius won't be around as much as Taurus might like.

Gemini human

A Gemini owner will really adore the Sagittarius cat, and will love the way it pounces and plays. There's no problem keeping the place in order because the dance between these two will be perfectly timed and in just the right rhythm for both.

Cancer human

The Cancer person will be spending a large part of his or her time with the Sagittarius cat, trying to tame it. That's a bit futile because Sagittarius is no ordinary kitty; it's naturally wild and free, really and needs to be left to be itself.

Leo human

Both of these two Fire sign creatures are bestial, and the Sagittarius cat will have no choice but to be well behaved when the domineering but friendly Leo owner instills some rules. Leo is perhaps the only star sign that Sagittarius will be tamed by.

Virgo human

Being at odds with one another, they'll see each other as foreigners. The Virgo person and the Sagittarius cat could become terribly frustrated with each other, so thank heaven for the great outdoors where they can each occasionally escape.

Libra human
The Libra person prefers a lively cat to a languid one, and although the Sagittarius cat can be a little unruly, the Libra individual is so good-humored and naturally in love with this cat that it won't be a problem, especially if they have a garden.

Scorpio human
The Libra cat could become frightened of the Scorpio person every once in a while, but so would anyone—it will just have to get used to it. There's love between these two and truthfully, neither would ever do anything to harm the other.

Sagittarius human
"Meow?" More like "Yeow!" This is one high-spirited couple. How do they manage to keep a home? Someone from the civilized world will have to come in every once in a while to put it back in order. There's never a dull moment here.

Capricorn human
The Sagittarius cat will learn to be more careful around the Capricorn person, honestly. There are boundaries resembling 12-foot high walls. This cat will get tired of trying to scale them, so it'll find another way around, like an open window.

Aquarius human
With so many vibes and electric currents passing through the unseen environment of the Aquarius home, the Sagittarius cat will have no time to climb walls. It is mesmerized by its Aquarius owner and there's great mutual respect.

Pisces human
Although the Pisces person will adapt to the untamed ways of the Sagittarius cat, there will be other times when this smart kitty will push things too far and Pisces will wind up in tears. Never mind, there's always tomorrow.

Capricorn

Suggested names for the Capricorn cat

Abraham, Abe, Marshall, Diablo, Hershey, Snowy, Glacier, Fonzie, Frosty, Moses, Edmund, Hillary, Roosevelt, Cool

Famous cat most likely to have been Capricorn

Garfield

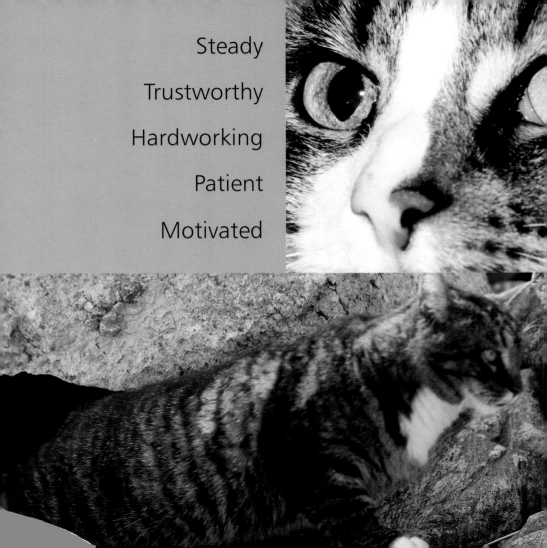

Steady

Trustworthy

Hardworking

Patient

Motivated

The Capricorn cat is the big daddy of them all! This creature simply oozes an innate authority that makes other cats balk at the prospect of initiating a play fight, just in case it turns into a real one. Even when young, the Capricorn kitten behaves like a mature cat. It seems to have more common sense than most other kitties. It's a little slower, deliberate in its movements, and not always in a playful mood. It takes the business of learning the skills required to become a proper cat very seriously. These are mainly about hunting and survival, but when it's not engaged in such active pursuits the Capricorn cat recognizes the need to conserve energy, and will spend an equal amount of time relaxing and resting.

What all this means is that your Capricorn feline is something of a loner, and so self-contained and self-sufficient that others avoid it for fear of receiving a frosty reception. But it has a playful side: it occasionally acts the clown and would be thoroughly bemused to know that it gives off a "keep your distance" vibe. Distant? It was just playing it cool, not trying to be as hard as nails! Still, this is probably not the best cat to choose as a pet for smaller children.

Capricorn cat needs to make a thorough investigation of its environment as well; it just likes to know where it stands, but you may get a tad annoyed with the way it's always poking around. As ever, be gentle with your feline companion because it so easily gets hurt feelings. The Capricorn cat can be very sensitive to scolding, and takes it seriously. So, although it might appear that it's sulking when it refuses to look at you or turns its back on you, that's just your perception. The Capricorn cat knows exactly what you mean when you say "No." It knows when it has been naughty and is respectful of your commands simply because you are bigger than it is. It is a cat's natural reaction to avert its gaze when it's being told off, so the Capricorn cat is not being snooty or stuck up, just dutiful—it recognizes that you have more authority in the household hierarchy than it does.

This cat is a natural born climber. It takes every opportunity to scale the heights and enjoys looking for advantageous places to perch. So it's not unusual to find it on the top of your closet, or bookcase, or up a tree. And it won't be up there because it was chased by the neighbor's dog: it simply prefers the vantage point that being up high affords. Plus, it likes the challenge and the sense of accomplishment it feels once it's there. So, except for the rare occasions when you're calling out the firefighters with their

extra-long ladders, let it be—the Capricorn cat knows precisely what it's doing. Why does it like a panoramic view? So that it can survey the area and spot more prey, of course. The Capricorn's mode of hunting is all about strategy; it likes to be clued up about where its prey is most likely to appear and in which direction it's most likely to bolt.

All cats have an inborn instinct to hunt—that's why they appear to play with their prey before killing it. Like any cat, your Capricorn moggy won't always go after birds and mice just to enjoy a fresh meal. Even when it's well fed, a cat needs something to chase, and if it doesn't happen to live in a tailor-made hunter's playground, it will make the game of physical pursuit last for as long as it can. It's really not as sadistic and cruel as some humans think. Your cat is just being its innate self by going after other small animals.

When sleeping, the Capricorn cat would prefer to be positioned high up. This is easy if you have a home with an upper floor and flight of stairs; in that case a basket or box on the landing, from where it can see down the stairs, will be perfect. On the other hand, if your living quarters are on one level, then your Capricorn cat will often be found sleeping on the headrest of your sofa, or even on the kitchen countertop. Cold and hard, you might think? Comfort is really a secondary consideration for the Capricorn cat—a vantage point and a good view mean so much more.

The Capricorn cat can put away as much food as a Taurus or Cancer cat yet never look as though it has eaten a decent meal in all its nine lives. And it won't be the slightest bit fussy or finicky about what you give it. Standard cat food will be just fine when it needs to refuel. Lean and lithe, all the calories it takes in are immediately converted into sinewy muscle. This is one of the longest-lived cats around. But in later life, when it starts slowing down and restricts its climbing to the lower branches, the Capricorn cat will start to put on weight. When that happens, it will use its size rather than speed to gain the respect it feels is its due.

Respect is extremely important to the Capricorn cat. It can go without lots of stroking and cuddles or time spent playing with its human owner. But you must always show this feline respect, praise it for its achievements, and feed it regularly. Do that, and you'll have a quietly devoted companion that doesn't require any molly-coddling or pampering. A Capricorn is the perfect low-maintenance cat for the busy career person who needs some feline grounding during time out.

Compatibility

Aries human

The Capricorn cat won't exactly excite an Aries human, who is a bit of a thrill seeker. On the other hand, it may be the only living creature that the Aries person will allow to lead by example with the innate authority of its calm, wise ways.

Taurus human

These two earthy creatures will rub along quite nicely together. The partnership will allow the Capricorn cat to develop a strong taste for style and luxury, so it may start resembling a proud Leo cat when it has a Taurus person by its side.

Gemini human

Eventually, these two may end up ignoring each other, which will upset the Gemini owner who likes to have lots of breezy little conversations and a little fun—behavior that the Capricorn cat will find rather silly and highly irritating.

Cancer human

Although on most levels these two will forge a thorough and complete understanding of each other, the Capricorn cat doesn't always appreciate the kind of loving affection that its Cancer human has to offer. But it will certainly love the food!

Leo human

The Capricorn cat won't let the Leo person down when it comes to displaying a sense of lofty self-containment and personal authority, but it can seem a little too cold for this warm hearted human.

Virgo human

This is a very nice arrangement, and these two get along really well. The Capricorn cat is sensitive to the needs and expectations of a Virgo person and will fulfill its catly duties with a strong sense of feline professionalism that not only impresses but also inspires.

Libra human

Although the lean, mean physique of the Capricorn cat appeals to Libra's aesthetic taste, this cat will not be impressed by any attempts to gild the lily. It will flatly refuse to wear any bows or frills—though a smart collar will be tolerated.

Scorpio human

With two such self-contained creatures, it's hard to imagine on what level they will cross personal boundaries to reach each other, but they will. Firstly through respect, and then through the slow drip-drip of Scorpio's psychic power.

Sagittarius human

The Capricorn cat will really start warming to the Sagittarius person after it realizes that this person won't be in the least bit petty about any bad behavior. As telling off will be kept to a minimum, friendship grows to the max.

Capricorn human

Respect for each other's boundaries will ensure that these two get on very well together. They may even become quite playful and have more fun than they could with anyone else, as both have a rather dark, ironic sense of humor.

Aquarius human

The Capricorn cat is no comic, but it will amuse an Aquarius person. Unfortunately, it's unlikely to work the other way round, as some of the more eccentric qualities of Aquarius could leave this cat feeling as if it's standing on shaky ground.

Pisces human

This is an excellent feline companion for the vague, dreamy, Pisces owner. The consistent adherence to the practicalities of daily life displayed by the Capricorn cat will help Pisces to find a gentle but firm path back down to earth.

Aquarius | 21 January to 19 February

Aquarius

Suggested names for the Aquarius cat

Dude, Freakie, Kinky, Gadget, Gizmo, Neutron, Lincoln, Frater, Friend, Lewis, Starlight, Ganymede

Famous cat most likely to have been Aquarius

The Cheshire Cat

Alert

Lively

Outgoing

Intelligent

Gregarious

The Aquarius cat won't be the one hassling for attention around your ankles or jumping on your lap for a little extra stroking—it's the coolest cat of the bunch. However, it is genuinely fascinated by humans and will tend to hang around, watching what you're doing. It's really on a quest to find out a little more about us two-legged folk, so that it can clue up all its cat friends about those weird, mysterious human creatures.

At times, you might think that you're being studied by a little scientist doing experiments. The Aquarius cat's idea of a good time would be to set you up with a prank, like leaving your belongings in the middle of the floor. It just wants to watch you trip over them and observe your behavior—the way you fall, your emotional reaction, and the way you stand up again. That amuses it. So from this point of view, your cat might appear to be more sociable than it really is. Sure, it'll go down the alley and find its pals, shoot the breeze, and pass on whatever it's learned, but there's usually some added agenda such as mating or marking its territory—natural kitty pastimes.

The Aquarius cat is a seeker. It does enjoy company, stimulation, and, yes, sometimes just plain socializing with animals or humans, but it prefers the role of spectator to that of participant. So it doesn't really make it as the greatest hunter among the feline fraternity. Not enough practice. It loves the encounter with all other creatures in the world, and it might bite, play, and at times even kill a mouse, but it has a more casual approach to these activities. The Aquarius cat doesn't get emotionally involved.

Have you ever noticed how some cats ask to be let indoors only

91

seconds after being let outdoors or vice versa? This can happen endless times a day—and that's why the cat flap was invented. Actually, it was probably first created for an Aquarius cat—for no other reason than that it is a true freedom lover.

Somewhere in the psyche of the original cat is a desire for the liberty to roam wherever it pleases. Therefore, these doors that humans use to separate one room from the other really annoy it—much more than the irritation caused to humans by having repeatedly to let their cat in and then out. The Aquarius cat just isn't into doors. It would prefer it if everything were open. That way it could sleep when and where it liked, come and go as it pleased, and eat when it chose to eat.

This is one of the most unpredictable and puzzling cats ever known to humankind. For months it'll be happy to do nothing but sit on the window ledge and watch the world go by, ignoring you and everything else that's going on inside the house. Then one day, for no apparent reason, you won't be able to sit down and watch your favorite soap on the television without your Aquarius cat deciding that there is something much more educational on the other channel. Once it gets its paws on the remote, you'll be shocked at how competently it changes channels. The point is that you won't be able to do a thing without your Aquarius cat poking its nose in. It's like this with food as well. Just when you think you've hit on its favorite meal of freshly prepared chicken livers and gravy, it'll suddenly switch and won't touch anything that hasn't come out of a tin. There's nothing quite like an Aquarius cat to keep you guessing.

The sleeping arrangements made by the Aquarius cat are just as wacky. It is important that you provide it with a designated bed, whether this is a basket, box, or some other bundle of coziness. It won't use it every night, preferring to sleep wherever it feels is most appropriate at the time. This may be your bed, a visiting guest's bed, or even the kitchen table; but woe betide you if after months of disuse you decide to clear some space and get rid of its bed. Your Aquarius cat will spend the entire night prowling around the house, looking for it and kicking up an enormous fuss. It's not that it's being possessive; it simply needs the security of having its permanent bed there for those moments when it wants to pretend to you and to itself that it's just an ordinary cat.

Don't you believe it! This is an extraordinary creature. All its observations of the world and conversations with other cats in the neighborhood have contributed to its powerful abilities of deductive reasoning. It will know the difference between the smell of smoke from a barbecue and that from a piece of electrical apparatus that's on fire. It'll be the first to scoot around and raise the alarm, gathering all the local cats, and even some dogs, to its cause, alerting everyone to the danger. It may not be emotional in the way it goes about its business, but the Aquarius cat doesn't like to see anyone get hurt. It'll stand up for those that can't stand up for themselves, and offer a paw in friendship to every stray it comes across, be it feline, canine, or human.

Having an Aquarius cat around is never straightforward—at times, it's the easiest cat in the world and at others just plain weird. But it'll be a good friend when you need it, and you can't say fairer than that.

Compatibility

Aries human

A perfect match. The Aquarius cat knows to stay well out of the way, especially when the Aries owner is rushing about to get to work or a party. Although there may be times when mealtimes are late or forgotten, they'll really get one another.

Taurus human

There'll be teething problems, not just at the beginning of this relationship, but in the middle and end, as well. But the Aquarius cat will learn that, as folks go, the Taurus person is not a bad provider and will see to its physical needs.

Gemini human

The Gemini owner will be thoroughly entertained by this quirky kitty, and it will feel that it has hit the jackpot with this attentive human. There's hardly a more suitable match for both of these bright and cheerful creatures.

Cancer human

The Aquarius cat could become bored in the Cancer household, though it will keep coming back for some of that home cooking! Plenty of air and outdoor space will make things easy for both.

Leo human

The one person who the Aquarius cat will really long for is its Leo owner. They'll give each other the freedom that each needs but when they're together they really love each other's company, so much that there's real resistance against either leaving.

Virgo human

For the Aquarius cat life is a little too precise in the Virgo home. Maybe the Aquarius kitty doesn't want to be back by 6 p.m. on the dot every day in order to get a fresh meal. Why can't it be served when it wants to come back instead?

Libra human

These two were made for each other. Light and breezy, this relationship requires no effort on either part because everything happens exactly as they expect of one another. Over time, their bond grows even closer.

Scorpio human

If there's one person who may become a target for revenge from an Aquarius cat, it's Scorpio—because Scorpio's intensity gets focussed onto this otherwise happy cat. There's no real harm done, but the atmosphere can get strained.

Sagittarius human

A mutual admiration society. And what follows the mutual admiration is mutual adoration. Not everyone is capable of understanding an Aquarius, let alone an Aquarius cat, but the Sagittarius person will make a pretty good job of it.

Capricorn human

This is a compelling relationship, like love and hate. If they spoke the same language, the airwaves would be filled with neverending rounds of bickering and then silence. Still, they won't be able to leave each other alone. There is love.

Aquarius human

It wouldn't be unusual to see the zany Aquarius owner pouncing around, acting like the perfect feline, while the Aquarius cat becomes the human being, looking perplexed at such odd behavior. A lot of kookiness goes on behind closed doors.

Pisces human

These two creatures are really very different, and yet they always seem to tantalize one another, and that's what keeps this relationship happy. They don't need to speak; they'll manage to understand what the other needs and wants.

Pisces | 20 February to 20 March

Pisces | The Dreamer

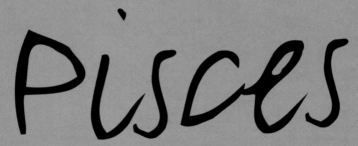

Suggested names for the Pisces cat

Infinity, Poppy, Poptart, Spirit, Sneaky, Xanadu, Bacardi, Nirvana, Dusty, Einstein, Flaky, Mystic, Marley, Sabbath

Famous cat most likely to have been Pisces

Bagpuss

Gentle

Sensitive

Intuitive

Dreamy

Emotional

The Pisces cat might seem to do nothing else but sleep, but that's just during the daytime—what it gets up to during the night is anyone's guess! But even if you're up at some dark hour and happen to run into your Pisces kitty, you'll never find out what it has been doing. It will sense you coming well before you arrive, and as you approach it'll sit there with the most sweet and innocent look on its face. You'll sense that it was up to something, but you'll never know what it was. Just adopt the mantra that what you don't know won't hurt you, and that'll be fine for both of you.

Truly, this is the most delightfully placid and pleasant of cats. It's quiet, unassuming, and rarely demands much. In fact, you could very easily forget it's there, because it has such a habit of staying out of your way. At times, you might think that this cat has gone missing: it has

a way of disappearing for long periods of time. Don't worry—the chances are that it vanished into the woodwork because it likes to drift away to other realms of cat heaven. One possible reason for these "absences" is too much catnip. This herb grows in the wild, so if it's not getting it at home, it'll find it elsewhere, and can easily become addicted to it. Everyone loves to see a cat go scatty over a little sachet of catnip, and the Pisces cat will love it, too. However, do remember that catnip is the feline equivalent of a drug—too much is not good.

Easygoing and eager to please, the Pisces cat will eat just about anything you give it. It rarely kicks up a fuss at mealtimes, and will be happy to fit in with your schedule. The only time you're likely to have it screeching around your ankles demanding to be fed is partially its own fault. You've probably become so used to thinking that it has disappeared somewhere, or been catnapped, or drifted into some other person's home and forgotten the way back, that you have stopped putting food out.

Have you seen people scurrying around the neighborhood at dinner time asking anyone and everyone whether they've caught a glimpse of their Pisces cat? When they get back, they'll find that it has been at home and asleep under the bed the whole time. So, while it's true that it may have wandered off into the horizon, with nine lives to live, this cat will always return home.

Even when the Pisces cat is providing you with obvious evidence of its physical presence, sitting in the middle of the room, or in clear view on the window ledge, it appears more like an apparition than a real, flesh, fur, and blood cat. It's so silent and graceful, flowing up and down over the furniture and around the house—it's as though it were made from some gravity-defying liquid. There is something quite hypnotic about watching a Pisces cat.

This feline doesn't give you the opportunity to watch it often as it's very shy and doesn't go in for big displays of extrovert behavior. You could sit for hours trying to observe it, camouflaged in long grass, softly stalking some prey that it has got its eye on, but never see the moment of the pounce. That always seems to happen the moment you've turned your head away for a second or got distracted by something else. And it's a rare Pisces cat that will bring home its catch for you. It seems to know that you're not really glad to have the proceeds of its hunt messing up your carpet.

This cat doesn't get off on insincere loud praise and clapping. The Pisces feline prefers quiet, gentle displays of affection. It's attracted to you most when you're engaged in a moment of reflection. When you sit and stare out of a window, your Pisces pet will come flowing to your side, gingerly placing a paw in your lap to test whether its presence will find favor. If you react, it'll probably move away, but if you stay still, then your Pisces cat will simply mold itself into your lap, creating as little disturbance as possible. This is a moment of pure bliss for the Pisces puss. It is connecting with you, its favorite human, on a level that neither of you has to think about too much. This is the ultimate bonding experience. It's also very trusting, which is why you'll often find it rolling over belly-up when it sees you coming. It wants you to know that it's all yours—at that moment anyway. It won't do this with strangers, so it's truly flattering to know that it really loves you.

Your Pisces cat won't need much in the way of toys, except when it's a kitten. Nothing is quite so cute as a Pisces kitten playing with a ball—it's fascinated by the way it rolls around. That's probably how it learned to flow seamlessly across a floor itself. As it gets older though, the Pisces cat won't go in for games, but a scratching post will go down very well, particularly if it is in the same room as the stereo. Music holds a special attraction for the Pisces cat, who will naturally drift toward the sounds of a lilting melody as though drawn by some unseen power.

It won't be as playful as a Gemini, as exciting as an Aries, or as affectionate as a Cancer, but the Pisces cat has some other great magical quality that makes it a very desirable feline friend. You may never know what it is, but once you've experienced it you'll never want to be without it.

Compatibility

Aries human

A case of opposites attract. The dreamy, fluid Pisces cat will fascinate an Aries person—whenever kitty happens to be awake, that is! However, living with the over-the-top energy of an Aries will ensure that being awake is something this cat avoids even more than usual.

Taurus human

By adopting a totally relaxed, but pragmatic, approach, the Taurus person will provide the Pisces cat with more ways to get chummy and close, so it will feel safer and tend to be a lot less shy.

Gemini human

While the Gemini person will admire the grace of a Pisces cat, and in return be rewarded with more interest than this cat would normally give to another living, nonfeline soul, neither of them has a clue where the other is coming from.

Cancer human

Provided the Cancer human doesn't make too much of an effort trying to forge an emotional bond with the Pisces cat, over time Pisces kitty will become less reticent and will freely offer the love and spooky silent connection they both need.

Leo human

A flashy, dramatic Leo provides more entertainment than the Pisces cat gets from other people, but its way of showing appreciation is a satisfied yawn at the end of a performance! This will be totally misread by the Leo who requires lots of applause.

Virgo human

As long as the impeccably clean and tidy Virgo isn't easily spooked or annoyed to discover the Pisces kitty snoozing among the bedlinen in the laundry basket, these two will develop a highly complementary and harmonious relationship.

Libra human

Nothing will delight this owner quite as much as having another graceful creature lazing about the elegant Libran home. The Pisces cat won't offer much intellectual stimulation, but the "look" will be absolutely purrfect, darling!

Scorpio human

This energetic Scorpio owner may try to make a Pisces cat behave more like a "proper" cat—stalking, hunting, pouncing, etc. However, the passive resistance, evidenced by the way the Pisces feline disappears at these moments, is too strong.

Sagittarius human

With a live and let live attitude being upheld by both the Sagittarius human and the Pisces cat, you'd think these two would get along much better. It's not that they don't get on—more a case that they don't see each other often enough.

Capricorn human

The Pisces cat really seems to amuse its Capricorn owner, but since it doesn't *do* very much it's hard to understand how. The Pisces cat must know, because it's always more than happy to curl up next to its Capricorn companion.

Aquarius human

Aquarians never think that they're making a connection with a Pisces cat, try as they might. What they don't realize is that all the bonding is taking place at a time when they're asleep and the Pisces cat is pouncing around in their dreams.

Pisces human

This is an excellent relationship, though from the outside it's hard to describe how this is possible, since they both seem to drift past each other without even noticing the other's presence. An unseen, unspoken bond.